JOHN I. SNYDER

SHELTERED
with
GOD

FINDING GOD'S PEACE IN A WORLD OF FEAR

A THEOLOGY MIX DEVOTIONAL

SHELTERED WITH GOD
FINDING GOD'S PEACE IN A WORLD OF FEAR

Copyright © 2020 by John I. Snyder
All rights reserved.

ISBN (eBook): 978-1-7359396-0-5
ISBN (Paperback): 978-1-7359396-1-2

A Book from Theology Mix | theologymix.com
Cover and Interior Design By: DPA Productions
Cover Image: Shutterstock

Trust in the Lord forever, for the Lord God
is an everlasting rock.
–Isaiah 26:4

In thankfulness to God for his mercy and protection.

He who dwells in the shelter of the Most High will abide in the shadow of the Almighty. I will say to the Lord, "My refuge and my fortress, my God, in whom I trust." For he will deliver you from the snare of the fowler and from the deadly pestilence. He will cover you with his pinions, and under his wings you will find refuge; his faithfulness is a shield and buckler.

–Psalm 91:1-4

And the peace of God, which surpasses all understanding, will guard your hearts and your minds in Christ Jesus.

–Philippians 4:7

CONTENTS

PREFACE

It seems like every time we turn on the news or check our social media streams, some new, terrible, heartbreaking event is taking place. Our world is changing, and it's changing rapidly. It's angry. It's scared. Many are full of fear. Even many longtime believers and faith warriors are experiencing times of uncertainty. What will happen? Where is God? Is he even listening?

If that's what you're asking in your situation, I want you to remember two things.

One: You are not alone. In my book *Resenting God*, I listed many Bible heroes who had expressed open frustration about the apparent "earlessness" of God. If they felt that way, we will, too. It doesn't mean it's true, but it is normal.[1]

Two: Our fears and frustrations have an antidote—Truth. The Truth. God's Truth. The same as it has been since the dawn of time, so it is today, in our darkness, in our fears, in our anxieties, our depression, our addictions. Let's not run from our fears, and let's certainly not let them control us. As believers we are called to live boldly—with power, strength, and surpassing joy.

For most of 2020, as the world has sheltered in place, we

have also been sheltered with God. This looks different for everyone, because God designs unique experiences for each one of us. Maybe we've discovered things about our lives that needed to change. Maybe it has stirred up new fears or created problems we did not think we would be facing. For most of us, it has done both.

Whatever the case, God has ordained this time for us— not to harm us, but for our good. Discovering that, and *living* it with joy and boldness, is what *Sheltered With God* is all about.

Will we go on to live without a moment of fear in our lives? Of course not. But through Christ's power, we can live without letting those fears reign over us and control our lives.

So let's do something different before we start this journey. First, let's focus in on our fears themselves and then ask ourselves, What is it that we are really seeking? To be closer to God? To overcome our current situation? To bring healing to us, or a relationship, or a loved one? Then let's pray together for God's message, God's peace, and God's joy to flood and fill our hearts and minds.

Are you ready for a life without fear?

ROOM 506: LESSONS FOR LOCKDOWN

This God—his way is perfect;
the word of the LORD proves true;
he is a shield for all those who take refuge in him.
For who is God, but the LORD?
And who is a rock, except our God?
–Psalm 18:30-31

We were supposed to be flying from San Francisco to New York.

The day before we were set to leave, my wife Shirin tripped over a concrete parking lot block, came crashing down, and wrenched her ankle. Not one to stay down, she picked herself up and limped over to meet our daughters Sarah and Stephanie in the nearby computer store, and they called to tell me what had happened.

My wife is a strong, brave woman. When I get sick, I'm a victim of the virulent Man Flu, whereas she can withstand just about anything with grace and poise. So she played down the fall with several "I'm fines," and at the time, we didn't know the extent of her injuries.

A trip to the emergency room revealed a bad break that caused us to cancel all travel plans. Room 506 at a local motel near the airport, intended to be our stopover for only two nights, turned out to be our home for the next *seven weeks*.

This already sounds like the beginning of a reality TV show! Generally, the physical circumstances were not all that bad, since we had a wonderful view of the San Francisco Bay. From our fifth-floor outdoor walkway we could watch the planes taking off and landing at the airport just a few miles away. The scene at night was spectacular. Sure, it was tight, but almost immediately things began to happen that cause us now to look back on that experience as one of those serendipitous times in the life of our family.

Endless hours of forced rest and reflection after a whirlwind of ministry activity in Europe led to many hours of writing and editing books, something for which we had little time before.

This also became a particularly joyful chapter of our lives. We had to work together very closely to make sure everything was coordinated, from meals to laundry—endless details needed to be taken into account and each of us had our particular part to play. We learned to depend on God and on each other, and to enjoy it as an adventure.

And the blessings didn't end there. Good friends we hadn't seen in years came to visit us, and to make sure Shirin had everything she needed to recover. God also granted our family great favor in the eyes of the motel staff and we were deeply blessed by their loving generosity and kindness.

We got to know the many personal stories behind their lives at the motel. Women and men from Cambodia, Panama, Peru, China, Mexico, and many other places all had accounts of refugee camps, escapes from dangerous countries and hostile governments, injuries and sicknesses, great struggles through which they passed before getting their motel jobs. They were not strangers or foreigners. They were Lara, Mary, Mateo, and Bao, brothers and sisters with children to educate, bills to pay, and personal challenges to overcome.

Above all, a clear advantage of spending so much time in room 506 was the bonding of our family. In the midst of the difficulties we were facing, and there were plenty of them, we learned the lesson again that if a family lives in love for one another, then it really doesn't matter where they are or what the circumstances are. The humblest one-room dwelling can be a very blessed home, or the most modest budget can be more than enough, if we live in an environment of affection and mutual respect. We already knew this, but it helped to have it confirmed once more in a time of confusion and struggle.

As we have lived through a pandemic, divinely reunited together in a small apartment in Munich, Germany, we thank God for the training we received years ago for a time like this. We know the drill and realize this is not the worst storm our family has ever faced together. But it is an opportunity to witness how God takes the bad things that happen to us and turns them into the best things that happen to us. No matter how severe or devastating our life storms, God is still able to use them for his good purposes and our welfare. This is something we can't really know until we actually go through them and come out joyous on the other side to tell others of God's rescues and good provisions.

Are you in the middle of a life storm right now? God is teaching you something. It may be unpleasant for the moment, but as someone on the other side, I can tell you—wait. Wait for God. He is doing something that you can't see right now, but it will amaze you later. That's a reason to live without fear today.

BEGINNING PRAYER

Heavenly Father, you know this pandemic has been a great struggle—a time of heartache and loss, anxiety and stress for me and many others—but with you everything can become a blessing. I pray this will end soon, but that in the meantime you will show me how you bring good out of evil, and my welfare out of confusion and pain. Use this as a time of spiritual awakening, for me and for those around me, for Jesus' sake. Amen.

FACING FEAR WITH FAITH

When I am afraid,
I put my trust in you.
In God, whose word I praise,
in God I trust; I shall not be afraid.
What can flesh do to me?
–Psalm 56:3–4

These are extraordinary times. The coronavirus pandemic has raged through our planet, sending the entire world into lockdown. Protests have hit the streets internationally. Hearts are broken. Peace and goodwill seem a distant dream.

We have witnessed the impact of all this. People are afraid. The dawn of lockdown had masses panic buying and stockpiling. People are angry, lashing out at each other and defying common courtesy. Fear and defeat are stamped on the faces of so many. What is happening is shocking and unbelievable!

How then should we approach this without fear?

We as believers have a special responsibility in these days. What we need to keep in mind, above everything else, is that we are the people of God, bearing witness to the

Kingdom, and living before our neighbors as those whose citizenship is in heaven, not on this earth.

History reminds us that the world has been through many such things before, even much worse, and come out victorious. In the 14th century, the Black Plague ravaged Europe with astronomical casualties. But there were many in one group of people who managed to escape the brunt of it—these were the people of God, the Jews. Due to the anti-Semitism of their time, they were blamed for the Plague and further persecuted. However, paying careful attention to their *Torah* (the first five books of the Old Testament), they scrupulously followed what they understood as God's instructions on cleanliness. By following specific hygiene rules, they were able to prevent sickness and death.

The Jews didn't know why their lives were spared. The germ theory of disease was not widely known or accepted. But they were sure of one thing—God's words needed to be followed, and God's commands were to be obeyed at all costs, and without challenge.

There is something we can learn from this. We have very clear instructions from both Testaments that as Christians, we are to be completely trusting in our God. We are actually commanded to be free from panic and fear! In the Gospel of Matthew, Jesus directly commands us, "Therefore do not be anxious about tomorrow, for tomorrow will be anxious for itself. Sufficient for the day is its own trouble" (Matthew 6:34).

This might seem easier said than done. Remember, it's a

command that, like all his great commands, can be kept only as we "abide"—dwell, rest confidently—in him (John 15:5). We can do nothing on our own strength. The apostle Paul affirms that because of Christ we are to be anxious about nothing—not anxious about very little, or anxious about almost nothing, but anxious about *nothing*—because Jesus will keep us in the peace of God (Philippians 4:4–7). Read that again. Jesus will keep us in the peace of God. We are sheltered with him.

When we follow the words of Jesus with the same eye to detail as the people of God did for centuries, we will draw from his strength and power, and through this bear witness to a fearful and panicked world. They will look at us and see what fearlessness looks like. Through the power of the Holy Spirit, we can stare down disease, war, and even the fear of death itself.

We don't know what God is up to in allowing this disease to spread across the world, but we can be sure that he trains us to be the light shining on a hill to a world that has no such hope as ours. If there ever was a time to be real Christians, as part of a real church, and to light up the world illustrating the Kingdom of God, this is the time.

Let us heed the call to bring hope to the hopeless, praying for our neighbors and being given to the welfare of others over ourselves. The world needs the healing power of Christ in its time of pain and sorrow.

PRAYER

Almighty God, remind us that fear and anxiety are not what you want for us, and that you have a purpose for everything you allow to happen on this earth. Give us strength to obey your command not to worry. Redirect our attention from our own distress, and toward your will for your people in hard times. With this courage, let us give ourselves to the needs of others who don't know you and illustrate your Kingdom with joy and trust. Amen.

MY DAILY JOURNAL

WHERE IS GOD IN A
WORLD CRISIS?

"Remember this and stand firm,
recall it to mind, you transgressors,
remember the former things of old;
for I am God, and there is no other;
I am God, and there is none like me,
declaring the end from the beginning
and from ancient times things not yet done...."
–Isaiah 46:8–10

In times of fear and heartache, it's inevitable to ask where God is. Can he hear us? Will he help us? Is he personally involved in the crisis spreading across the world?

The Bible is absolutely clear on this. God is sovereign. He is in charge of everything that happens in history. He foreknows and oversees every event, great or small, good or bad, and has the last word on everything that occurs anywhere in his universe. Every day of our time here is held firmly in his hands. So to the question, "Where is God in this pandemic?" or "in this destructive and increasing hatred?" or "in this time of unrest?" or "in my heartbreak?" the answer is, "Right here, in the middle of it." He could have prevented it, he could stop it anytime he wishes, and he can bring out of it anything he desires. And he will.

The Bible explicitly tells us that his will is to enter into whatever evil is taking place on his planet and to rearrange things so that his predetermined good will come from it, "according to the plan of him who works out everything in conformity with the purpose of his will" (Ephesians 1:11). This summarizes the Bible's position on all of human history.

What, then, is the practical application of this "philosophy of history" to the current COVID-19 crisis, or any past or future crisis, affecting the entire world?

It means that God is in complete charge of it, whatever its source, and that he will exploit and bring out of it everything he chooses to accomplish in his many-sided purpose. We may not know right now what that is, but we can be sure that he knows.

We can be confident that God will bring to pass in this strange time what he manages to do in every flood, earthquake, tsunami, war, or cataclysm of any sort: judgment for some, blessing for others, rescues, restorations, reversals of fortune, losses and gains, spiritual awakening for those who are asleep, and more. In time, such human stories will emerge, as they always do.

But for the moment, what's important for us to remember is that God, his character, and his purpose are the core issues at every point, because in a fallen world that chronically (and increasingly) wants God to be the center of nothing, he is actually the center of everything.

And even though we don't and can't know the whys and hows of this global event, we can and must pray day and night that he will rescue his world from this overt evil, while achieving all that he wants to extract from it. In the final analysis, our prayer is not only, "God help us, because we take refuge in you!" but, "Lord, let your will be done and your name be glorified."

Our role today, in the midst of a pandemic, in every crisis, is not to call into question God's character, or to demand an explanation for everything that occurs in his world, but to seek how we can be his instruments of help and reconciliation in the middle of it.

PRAYER

Dear God, help me understand that you alone are sovereign, that you are in charge of your universe, and that nothing happens in your world that surprises you or catches you off guard. Let me never forget that you are good, and you are the God who knows how to bring great good out of great evil, whatever it may be. Amen.

MY DAILY JOURNAL

GOD IN OUR MIDST

Five times I received at the hands of the Jews the forty
lashes less one. Three times I was beaten with rods. Once
I was stoned. Three times I was shipwrecked; a night and
a day I was adrift at sea; on frequent journeys, in danger
from rivers, danger from robbers, danger from my own
people, danger from Gentiles, danger in the city, danger
in the wilderness, danger at sea, danger from false
brothers; in toil and hardship, through many a sleepless
night, in hunger and thirst, often without food,
in cold and exposure.
–2 Corinthians 11:24–27

Are you feeling shipwrecked in your life? Do you wonder where God is when you need him most? You're not alone. Like others, you were following God's direction, but suddenly everything around you shut down or changed course. Now you're lost in a wilderness of doubt, feeling like Joseph tossed into the pit, despairing of a way out or of ever sensing God's pleasure, presence, and rescue in your life. Or maybe you feel the presence of God, but you're in a heavy fog and you can't see the way ahead.

As we see in 2 Corinthians, Paul faced some incredibly

difficult times—from shipwrecks to hunger, to being hunted down for his own life, he went through it all!

Let's face it, the Christian life can be as much of a rollercoaster ride as anyone else's. We as Christians have no immunity to life's problems or surprises. However, in page after page, the Bible assures us that we do have a faithful God who loves us and goes with us into, and through, each trial. I love this verse from Jeremiah: "…the Lord appeared to him from far away. I have loved you with an everlasting love; therefore I have continued my faithfulness to you" (31:3). What a powerful testimony to his love and faithfulness to us!

Unfortunately, the thorny path is what we need and what God uses to bring us into the likeness of his Son. We've heard this before, and during this time it may be the last thing we want to hear again. But it bears repeating. As we pass through each painful experience, each unexpected loop of life's wild and unpredictable ride, we learn to lean on God and, in turn, grow more Christlike, displaying the fruit of the Spirit: love, joy, peace, forbearance, kindness, goodness, faithfulness, gentleness, and self-control (Galatians 5:22–23).

But Paul assures us that whatever setback, sadness, or grief we may experience in this life is absolutely nothing—not even to be compared with—the glory that is to be revealed in our permanent future (Romans 8:18). C.S. Lewis in his *Chronicles of Narnia* series portrays our destiny as a book in which every chapter will be better than the last.

"Now at last they were beginning Chapter One of the

Great Story which no one on earth has read: which goes on for ever: in which every chapter is better than the one before."[2]

Is all this too good to be true? We could draw this conclusion if God was never actively present in our troubles and simply let us muddle painfully through them on our own. But the great, amazing fact of the Christian life is what we discover on our darkest days (or soon after)—that we are never alone, God has not forgotten us for a single moment, and has surrounded us with his Spirit and his angels to comfort, encourage, bless, and heal.

> The Lord your God is in your midst,
> a mighty one who will save;
> he will rejoice over you with gladness;
> he will quiet you by his love;
> he will exult over you with loud singing.
> –Zephaniah 3:17

So it is God's presence, his answers to prayer, his rescues, his arranging and rearranging of things, and all his surprises, that give us solid, reasonable grounds for believing in a better, hope-filled tomorrow. Whatever it looks like right now, we can move ahead with the confidence that no matter what we encounter along the way, God is already there. He will continue to escort us through today, and every day after that, so we can walk with the joy-filled boldness that in all our

ups and downs, gains and losses, we are in the hands of our
heavenly Father.

PRAYER

Lord God, I praise you that you know the end from the
beginning! Thank you that you are accomplishing your
good purposes for me, and that you are forever in our
midst. Grant me the strength to wait on you, to feel your
love and presence in my life as I try to push through my
pain and move forward toward the good you have
already determined for me. In Jesus' name, I pray.

MY DAILY JOURNAL

LIFE LESSONS AT THE UNIVERSITY OF ADVERSITY

As day was about to dawn, Paul urged them all to take some food, saying, "Today is the fourteenth day that you have continued in suspense and without food, having taken nothing. Therefore I urge you to take some food. For it will give you strength, for not a hair is to perish from the head of any of you." And when he had said these things, he took bread, and giving thanks to God in the presence of all he broke it and began to eat.
–Acts 27:33–35

In this chapter of Acts, it's clear that Paul was in a mess. But it was a divine mess.

The apostle Paul was hoping for a normal voyage on the ship, although he warned the captain that it wasn't wise to sail during the stormy season. He knew what he was talking about because he had already experienced three prior shipwrecks! He was overruled and off they went—the ship had a schedule to keep. But no one knew that God had other plans for this journey—an unscheduled stop on the island of Malta, where Paul was to carry out his ministry before moving on to Rome.

In this long passage from Acts 27, we learn of this interruption and the introduction to another, greater plan, conceived only in the mind of God. But by now, Paul was used to having things turned upside down as God led him on a different path. Another divine surprise! And the "twist in fate" was intended for Paul to understand what was really taking place and to learn how to look for signs of God's presence and leading.

Have you ever experienced what looks like God's personal involvement in your life? Anyone who has ever witnessed a clear-cut case of providence intersecting with their life tells more or less the same story of the way God intervenes. First, it points directly to him. It casts our eyes upward, so we look to our Maker and know he was the one who did this for us. Second, it is something only he can do. It shows his power, his authority, and his unwavering commitment to his will, for our good. Finally, and perhaps most impactful for us, it is personal. It shows that he is intimately involved in our lives, in such a way that his love for us is totally, extravagantly, overwhelmingly clear.

Many years ago on a lake in northern California, my father experienced a very strange and inexplicable event involving the outboard engine of his ski boat. It was something that wouldn't have had the slightest impact on the mind or heart of anyone else, but my dad was a master mechanic, and what happened persuaded him of God's personal interest in him.

When my dad first bought the family a new ski boat, he

made a vow to God that he wouldn't take the boat out on the lake on a Sunday and miss worship. However, there was this one Sunday when my brother Gary made a rare, quick visit to see my parents, so my dad decided, just this once, to treat him to a day on the boat.

They headed for the lake, and when they arrived my dad unhitched the boat, slid it into the water, and prepared to take my brother skiing. When he pushed the throttle to full forward, the engine wound up nicely, and then suddenly blew up with a loud popping noise.

Being a master of machines and supervisor of maintenance for a large airline, who could take apart and put together anything from a Boeing 747 to a tiny watch, he knew after careful inspection that the day was over. The outboard motor was frozen.

No sooner did the family return home than he took the engine apart piece by piece. He couldn't find any problem. Everything was in perfect order. He carefully put it back together and started it up in the garage. It ran like new.

It was at that exact moment he thought of the promise he had made to God. This mechanical anomaly put in his path occupied a place in his mind for the rest of his life. It was so personally designed, so uniquely tailor-made, that he knew that God was directly involved with him. He cared about my dad's promises.

Through such personal divine events, God demonstrates his nearness to us, usually in creative ways that would have little meaning to anyone else but maximum impact to the one meant to get the message. In the way parents love to surprise their children, he seems to love to create the unexpected, so that we'll rely increasingly more on him and less on "general principles" about guidance.

We like to write books on "The Three Steps," "The Four Principles," and "The Five Rules" of God's direction, but just when we think we've discovered a formula for how he works, he goes the other way and does something entirely different. We learn that he doesn't want to give us a formula at all. He wants to give us himself.

So what does this mean?

Simply this: God wants to be our guide, not to give us a roadmap. He wants us to trust *him*, not some set of rules or homemade superstitions. And it's at this point where we part ways with religion and live life by faith. Religion gives us rules, principles, rites, rituals, incantations, customs, and laws. But faith gives us someone to trust and love—a close connection with our heavenly Father.

To keep us from falling into just another religion of do's and don'ts, and to keep us in a living relationship, God constructs new and surprising (and often humorous) ways of leading us from point A to point B.

I strongly encourage you to read the New Testament account of Paul's "visit" to the island of Malta (Acts 27:1– Acts 28:10) because it serves as a model of how God so often leads us. On the surface of it, Paul and his entourage were just blown off course by a sea storm and driven onto a small, insignificant island. But as we read on, we discover that in this messy change of plans Paul had a divine appointment with some very specific people God had in mind from the very beginning. It didn't even look like guidance to many of those involved, but it turned out to be the clearest possible involvement of God in the midst of great danger and adversity.

Sometimes we find ourselves where we are because our ship sank and we washed up on the beach, dazed and soaking wet. It's in our long years of study at the University of Adversity where we learn some of our best life lessons. God's guidance will often be most obvious and dramatic during our life's storms, reversals, losses, and sorrows.

As I mentioned, over the years in ministry and foreign missions, much travel, frequent moving, dangerous situations, and opposition of all sorts and on all sides, what our family has learned is this: Some of the worst things that have ever happened to us have turned out to be some of the best things that have ever happened to us.

And often when we were in the middle of it, we thought that nothing worse could have happened, that God seemed to have abandoned us, he didn't care about us, that nothing made any sense at all. We complained long and hard about "shock fatigue" or the rotten set of circumstances he had given us, and we tried to persuade him that if he really were a loving heavenly Father, then he wouldn't have done this or that. But in the end, we finally got the point that he actually knows what he's doing and that he alone is in charge of our life (and the world) and we aren't. That's a very important graduation day. Amazingly, like any great teacher, God is overly patient with us as we learn.

The more we think about the many creative and unpredictable ways he discloses himself and guides us, the more we come to love and enjoy his character. The more we are dazzled by his ways.

Our God *is* an awesome God!

PRAYER

Lord, I am amazed at how creative you are in guiding me from one place to another. I so easily forget that I live by eternal purpose, not just by my hopes and wishes of the moment. I am surprised at trouble and tribulation that turn out to be for my good, and that my plans may have little to do with your great Plan. Like the apostle Paul, help me to ride the storm, and to discover what it is that in your grace and mercy you have decreed for me. Amen.

MY DAILY JOURNAL

WHY IS GOD DOING THIS TO ME?

For the Lord is good; his steadfast love endures forever, and his faithfulness to all generations.
–Psalm 100:5

G od moves in a mysterious way... Familiar words to all of us, even those outside the church. What is lesser known is the story behind the author of this famous hymn and the heartache he endured.

William Cowper was born in Berkhamsted, England, in 1731, the son of John Cowper, rector of the Church of St Peter. A life of tribulation and pain led to an attempted and failed suicide, and Cowper found himself admitted to St. Albans Insane Asylum. It was here that he happened to read Romans 3:25: "God presented Christ as a sacrifice of atonement, through the shedding of his blood—to be received by faith. He did this to demonstrate his righteousness, because in his forbearance he had left the sins committed beforehand unpunished" (NIV). This led to his conversion and an unshakeable faith (through a continued life of ups and downs) in God's sovereign power, his love, goodness, and faithfulness. He penned the famous "Light Shining Out of Darkness" that we know now as "God Moves in a Mysterious Way." This hymn has provided life-giving words of hope for believers to cling to when they are uncertain how the grief-stricken moments in their lives will turn out.

> *Blind unbelief is sure to err,*
> *And scan his work in vain;*
> *God is his own interpreter,*
> *And he will make it plain.*
> –**William Cowper**, *Light Shining Out of Darkness* [3]

When we run out of human theories about why this or that happens (or doesn't happen), we can rest in the truth that God's character never changes. In fact, we can trust in three truths:

- God's love
- God's goodness
- God's unfailing faithfulness

And we will discover, after going through the valleys and coming out safely on the other side, that we didn't need, and don't need, to know more than that.

Yet even before we find this out, during some of the lowest points in life, God in his mercy and care grants us insights into what is happening to us. This encouragement and understanding come from passages that give us reasons why God permits suffering in our lives. It is not because he doesn't care about us—it's because of his great love for us. God wants us to know that our suffering serves a positive role.

In 1 Peter 1, Peter writes to the church about suffering, with these powerful words:

> In this you rejoice, though now for a little while, if necessary, you have been grieved by various trials, so that the tested genuineness of your faith—more precious than gold that perishes though it is tested by fire—may be found to result in praise and glory and honor at the revelation of Jesus Christ (1 Peter 1:6–7).

Here is one of the keys to understanding trouble in the Christian life. No one has ever reached spiritual maturity without difficulties and resistance, usually lots of it. But it is God's way of propelling us toward "sainthood"—in other words, his highest will for us. We'll talk about this more in another chapter.

James tells us to count it "pure joy" when we meet different kinds of trials, "for you know that the testing of your faith produces steadfastness. And let steadfastness have its full effect, that you may be perfect and complete, lacking in nothing" (James 1:2–4).

In 2 Corinthians, Paul talks about one of his greatest troubles as a believer. Read his words from 2 Corinthians 12:

So to keep me from becoming conceited because of the surpassing greatness of the revelations, a thorn was given me in the flesh, a messenger of Satan to harass me, to keep me from becoming conceited. Three times I pleaded with the Lord about this, that it should leave me. But he said to me, "My grace is sufficient for you, for my power is made perfect in weakness." Therefore I will boast all the more gladly of my weaknesses, so that the power of Christ may rest upon me. For the sake of Christ, then, I am content with weaknesses, insults, hardships, persecutions, and calamities. For when I am weak, then I am strong (2 Corinthians 12:7–10).

God's power is made perfect in our weakness. So to our cry, "Why is God doing this to me?" we learn from these first Christians (Peter, James, Paul and the countless others who have experienced God's love and grace) that all the ups and downs, twists and turns, and everything else in this life have a reason and, ultimately, a very happy result. The goal of all this is our great, inexpressible joy, the gift that can never be taken away.

So let us say with King David: "Truly my soul finds rest in God; my salvation comes from him. Truly he is my rock and my salvation; he is my fortress, I will never be shaken" (Psalm 62:1–2, NIV).

PRAYER

Dear God, I'm sorry for misperceiving and misjudging your character and intentions for me. Forgive my complaining and accusing you, when all along you've done everything to bring about my maturity of faith and confidence in you. Put a new and right spirit within me, one that sees clearly your intentions for my ultimate joy. Amen.

MY DAILY JOURNAL

GOOD LORD, MORNING?

"For to the one who pleases him God has given wisdom
and knowledge and joy...."
–Ecclesiastes 2:26

How do you begin your day?

Do you wake up and jump out of bed, with an enthusiastic approach to what life is going to offer you today? A happy, "Good morning, Lord!" type of day? Or is it a "Good lord, morning?!" kind of experience?

Many of us have had the latter this year. But we're already hearing stories of some of the good things that have happened during the pandemic.

Project Wingman UK is an organization that was born out of it. Finding themselves laid off from their jobs, airline crew of every airline in the UK dedicated themselves to providing "First Class Lounges" for NHS staff and workers "to unwind, de-compress and destress before, during, and after hospital shifts." This was their way of honoring medical personnel risking their lives on the front lines of this pandemic war. Project Wingman has now expanded across the pond to the United States.[4]

We all need something to get us out of bed in the morning. In the middle of this pandemic (or any other season of suffering), the monotony of routine, no contact with others, and watching your resources dwindle can bring on depression and hopelessness, and it has for many people. So where are you spiritually, emotionally, and physically in this season of isolation?

Before you answer that, let's ask ourselves an unusual question: Does my misery make God happy?

We talk a lot about what makes *us* happy, how God can bring us joy, all the benefits of being part of the family of God, and more. But we don't stop and consider what makes God happy. (And no, I'm not trying to make this a guilt-trip!)

The surprising fact is that what makes God happy is aligned with what makes us happy! It's intended to bless our lives.

John tells us that God answers our prayers when we ask according to his will (1 John 3:22). So God isn't Santa Claus fulfilling your Christmas list. Instead, as believers, we ask because Jesus tells us to ask. But we also obediently accept that if what we ask will not be good for us, our request will not be granted. Instead, because of his favor toward us, God promises to give us what is for our best. In this spectacular, loving Father-child bond, we find that what delights God is at the same time the very thing that leads to our satisfaction and joy.

So if you can't face the morning, try to shout out praises to God, our heavenly Father. If you don't know what to say, read or cry aloud Psalm 100 (NIV):

> Shout for joy to the Lord, all the earth.
>   Worship the Lord with gladness;
>   come before him with joyful songs.
> Know that the Lord is God.
>   It is he who made us, and we are his;
>   we are his people, the sheep of his pasture.
>
> Enter his gates with thanksgiving
>   and his courts with praise;
>   give thanks to him and praise his name.
> For the Lord is good and his love endures forever;
>   his faithfulness continues through all generations.

This is our reason to get out of bed every morning, whether or not we feel like it at the time—we're here to love God. The only way to find fulfillment and joy is in pleasing God and enjoying who he is, for obeying his will and loving him is the key to a happy, meaningful life.

If today you feel no joy or are unable to praise God, he is not disappointed or surprised. You are his beloved child and he will bring you supreme joy and laughter to fill your life in his time and for your best. Like the crew at Project Wingman, often it comes only when we put love for others before our wants and needs.

PRAYER

Merciful God, even if I don't feel it right now, I thank you for this day, for every new morning you gift to me. Thank you for not granting me any of my requests that are not right for me. For all of the things that I want and need—from friendship to my literal daily bread—you know what they are, and you know how I am struggling. Help me to trust you while I wait, and give me the strength to seek your joy even in my pain. Give me the vision to see how I can help others you have put in my path, and grant me the wisdom to receive your will with a grateful heart. Amen.

MY DAILY JOURNAL

WHAT IF WE LOSE EVERYTHING?

Then Job arose and tore his robe and shaved his head
and fell on the ground and worshiped. And he said,
"Naked I came from my mother's womb, and naked shall
I return. The Lord gave, and the Lord has taken away;
blessed be the name of the Lord."
–Job 1:20–21

I heard about a man who spent his life building up three restaurants in New York City, who faced losing everything he possessed because his restaurants (except for take-outs and deliveries) had been shut down. Restaurants are one of the hardest-hit businesses during this time. They are another casualty of the coronavirus pandemic.

Sadly, this is not some rare exception. Many people—personally, professionally, and economically—stand to lose everything they have sacrificed for and built up over a lifetime. Rich, poor, and everyone in between are in peril of losing everything in a short period of time, with many already having done so.

But I'm a Christian. Isn't there some special protection for someone who lives for Jesus every day? God wouldn't let that happen to me, would he? The short answer is: Yes, he would, if that's his good purpose for you. And no, there's no "special protection," no tailor-made insurance policy that guarantees us an easier time than our next-door neighbor. It could be that God may choose to rescue you from this disaster, even prosper you in it, or he may allow you to go through the same thing that's happening to those around you. There is no protective bubble that necessarily surrounds Christians, making us immune to what everyone else is going through. History spells this out very clearly. The Bible says as much.

We may ask, then, *Where is our security? Why should we not be afraid of this pandemic?*

Our security lies in one fact: the guaranteed, history-proven promise of God to be with us in and through everything that happens in the world. If any believer is unaware of this, then this terrible virus, unfortunately, might be exactly what teaches the point.

Let's say that COVID-19 wipes out all your finances, everything you've worked for, saved, invested. Where are you then? You are where innumerable believers have found themselves for thousands of years—in the strong, secure hands of God. You learn what millions have already discovered, that *if you have God and nothing else, you have everything you need.*

The best way to look at this unexpected situation (as difficult as it may be) is as a phase in spiritual growth to see how God discloses himself as the Great Provider and

Protector the Bible says he is. And the Bible doesn't say these things just to sound good, or to make us feel warm and cozy, but because that's the whole point of thousands of years of accurate Bible history. It's called the "history of salvation." It describes the hundreds of ways God has chosen to rescue his people from disaster, death, and poverty, so we can't miss the point. And after you've experienced his mercy and grace in some remarkable way, then you can join the vast chorus of voices who joyfully sing his praises up to, and including, this day.

Have you asked to become an effective witness to his faithfulness in this critical time? He may grant the honor in a form you might not have expected: sickness, loss of a career or life savings, or something else, maybe even earthly life itself. Or maybe you didn't ask to become a witness at all. Perhaps you've never taken faith very seriously until faced with a crisis too big to handle, like the one right now.

For many of us longtime believers, we've been through it. We speak with authority when we say that just as there is nothing in this life that can't be taken away, so there is no loss that can't be restored in this life, or the next. This is one of the facts we learn from the Bible, and it works out this way only because God is the author of this classic plot.

Maybe we can approach our crises differently. Let's place our trust firmly in the One who said, "Have I not commanded you? Be strong and courageous. Do not be frightened, and do not be dismayed, for the Lord your God is with you wherever you go" (Joshua 1:9).

Let us lift our cries and prayers to a God who loves to answer in a way that leaves us stronger, more resilient, and with a more mature (and relevant) faith, the kind of faith the world needs to see.

PRAYER

Lord, I ask for the power of your Holy Spirit to make me strong and courageous in the face of heartache and loss. I look forward to seeing what you're going to make out of it. I know you are wise and good, and that you make all things work together for good to those who love you and are called according to your purpose. Let your will be done and show me what my role is in this drama, in Jesus' strong name, I pray. Amen.

MY DAILY JOURNAL

LIFE ON FURY ROAD

"Remember not the former things,
nor consider the things of old.
Behold, I am doing a new thing;
now it springs forth, do you not perceive it?
I will make a way in the wilderness
and rivers in the desert."
–Isaiah 43:18–19

Do you remember the post-apocalyptic action film *Mad Max: Fury Road*? It's basically two hours of adrenaline. From start to finish, it's a story of survival at any cost, with high-speed chases, explosions, giant vehicles with fire blazing out of them—it's a pretty exciting film.

It also seems like a good visual representation of how 2020 has gone for us!

Even in the midst of all these twists and turns—especially in the midst of them—it is time to remind ourselves that God is not a God of chaos, but of order, and of mercy and grace. As in the passage from Isaiah that we just read, he creates new things, a way in the wilderness, rivers in the desert.

This is one of those scriptures where God is explaining to Israel that even though they have been profoundly unfaithful to him, he is still faithful to them. God intends to restore all that was lost. This is good news for all of us, and in a way, we can be grateful for their example. Human nature never changes, and neither does God's. We should be perpetually thrilled there is nothing that can separate us from God's faithfulness to us.

Why does God insist on giving us this kind of hope and rescue? Just because that's who he is—the Holy One of Israel. It is the mark of his character, and by that alone, and nothing else, we are sure of his constant faithfulness, his rescuing power from every impossible situation, and his ability to open a door that doesn't even now exist. He can create a way out that we can't possibly even imagine. This means there is nothing to fear—not the future, not the past, not even our own mistakes.

Isaiah tells us that God can make a way in the wilderness and rivers in the desert. Both "wilderness" and "desert" capture the images that too many times describe our lives. Often by our own mistakes and sins, we lose our way, we end up in the desert of our own making, and then cry out to God whom we have disregarded and disobeyed. Amazingly, he comes to our rescue, after we've spent enough time in the sand and the heat to learn a few valuable lessons about real life. A priceless lesson we learn is that while we imagine that God is thousands of miles away from us, he is merely the distance of the nearest grain of sand, carefully watching over us.

The Psalmist gets it right when he extols the kindness

and righteousness of God toward the weary and lost:

> Some wandered in desert wastes,
>> finding no way to a city to dwell in;
> hungry and thirsty,
>> their soul fainted within them.
> Then they cried to the LORD in their trouble,
>> and he delivered them from their distress.
> He led them by a straight way
>> till they reached a city to dwell in.
> Let them thank the LORD for his steadfast love,
>> for his wondrous works to the children of man!
>> –Psalm 107:4–8

This history is both real and realistic and describes not only specific events in the Bible's "salvation history," but also portrays what has always happened, happens up to this present day, and will continue until the world's last day.

Without revealing any spoilers, *Mad Max* doesn't end in annihilation. The struggle does not go unrewarded, and the winding path, though filled with pain and strife, creates new strength, new friendships, and a new way in the wilderness. Whatever is going on in the world around us right now, we can celebrate the fact that God's stubborn faithfulness to his chosen beloved creatures will never, ever change.

PRAYER

Father, I really don't know all the whys of what has come my way. I am confused and frustrated, and I'm tired of trying to make things better without seeing any change. For the things that are simply out of my control...I leave them at your feet, knowing you love me and are working for me, not against me, with your power and grace. Thank you for remaining by my side despite my own unfaithfulness to you. Amen.

MY DAILY JOURNAL

FAITH IN THE FIRE

*In this you greatly rejoice, though now for a little while
you may have had to suffer grief in all kinds of trials.
These have come so that your faith—of greater worth
than gold, which perishes even though refined by fire—
may be proved genuine and may result in praise, glory
and honor when Jesus Christ is revealed.*
–1 Peter 1:6–7, NIV

I recently read a story about 33-year-old Iranian Ebrahim Firouzi, who has already spent over six years in prison. He is being held on charges including "propaganda against the Islamic regime, evangelism, contact with anti-Islamic agents abroad and running a Christian website." Even though he had served his sentence, he was further convicted of "actions against national security, being present at an illegal gathering and collusion with foreign entities." Even in his suffering, he still refused the judges' offers to dismiss the charges against him if he renounced his faith. He says prison taught him "endurance and submission."[5]

Our brother Ebrahim's story is similar to many followers of Jesus throughout history. In 1 Peter, the apostle was writing to believers who, even though they lived in the midst of the greatest miracles and revelations of God, yet endured some of the most horrific persecution. They were martyred in the cruelest ways imaginable. But they held fast to their faith. It gives us strength to know that the early church went through severe troubles, and if they hadn't, we might think that our experience in this world is an exception to the rule.

Peter makes two very helpful and encouraging points here.

First, whatever it is that's causing us pain, and however devastating it may be, it is *purely temporary*. It may for the moment be filling up the entire screen for us, but (unbelievable as it may seem) it is for the *moment*! And we may feel like our problems or grief will never end. But as sure as the sun rises each morning, there will come a day when it's all over and we can look back on our trial and either laugh at it or simply reflect upon it with a new sense of maturity and wisdom.

And even if it lasts until our last day on earth, we all know by now that time passes so swiftly that we always seem to say, "It went by so fast!" As a boy I discovered every year that the school term seemed painful and unending, but inevitably, the summer break with its promise of carefree, fun-filled days always arrived. So it is with our experience now.

Second, we can be assured that whatever the nature of our temporary troubles, God is using them to perfect us. This life is like the refiner's fire. The hotter it gets, the better it is for us. Like gold that is purified, we are being perfected by our suffering. We may not like this arrangement, for normally we want it easy, but that's not what grows us. Because of our fallen nature, we aren't likely to be matured and purified by more comfort, ease, and prosperity. We need the tough times.

Peter wants us to keep in mind that the whole point of this life is to grow in trust in a trustworthy God, and to spend a joyful eternity in his presence. So may our prayers not be simply, "Lord, make it easier for me," but, "Lord, fashion me into the image of Jesus your Son."

If you fear God has forgotten you and that you will never find your way out of your Maze of Misery, memorize these powerful words from Deuteronomy: "It is the Lord who goes before you. He will be with you; he will not leave you or forsake you. Do not fear or be dismayed" (31:8).

PRAYER

Lord, let me see you as clearly in my pain as I do in the many days of your happy blessings and pleasure. Grant me the great power by your Holy Spirit not only to come through this present fire with faith and even joy, but to emerge from it the strong and faithful disciple you've chosen me to be, for Jesus' sake, and your glory. Amen.

MY DAILY JOURNAL

_____

_____

_____

_____

_____

_____

_____

_____

_____

_____

_____

_____

_____

_____

_____

_____

OUR JOB DESCRIPTION: TO LIVE AND DIE FOR OTHERS

And Jesus called them to him and said to them, "You know that those who are considered rulers of the Gentiles lord it over them, and their great ones exercise authority over them. But it shall not be so among you. But whoever would be great among you must be your servant, and whoever would be first among you must be slave of all. For even the Son of Man came not to be served but to serve, and to give his life as a ransom for many."
–Mark 10:42–45

This saying of Jesus comes close to giving us our job description for earthly life, one that is completely opposite to what we're usually taught about how to be happy and fulfilled. When we strive to "lord it over all," Jesus teaches the contrary. If we are to follow Jesus, then we'll do what the Son of Man himself came into the world to do—to be a servant of all, to live and die for others. This is our calling and our vocation.

Jesus, the Man for others, gave his life for us. He died in our place for our sins; he paid the price that we couldn't pay. In doing so, he lived out his teaching that this is the key to human life in general. And this is exactly what millions have discovered over the centuries: True joy and fulfillment on this earth lie not in doing our own will and accumulating more riches and earthly treasures for ourselves, but in giving them and ourselves away to others.

Who are those who come to the end of life with a sense of having lived well and to the fullest? Who among us have the fewest hang-ups and neuroses, the least guilt, and fewest regrets? It's those who have willingly and joyfully given up the heavy burden of trying to fulfill themselves first, and moved boldly ahead into the task of helping, feeding, sheltering, rescuing, and loving others.

Some of the happiest people you will ever meet are those whose lives are spent in some form of sacrifice for others, who give their time and energies to the Gospel and to the work of lifting up those on the bottom rung of the ladder—physically, materially, or emotionally. Joy is found in giving rather than taking. This is one of life's greatest secrets, and it gives us a clue to how we are actually wired. It may seem to most people upside down, because it goes against much of what our culture tells us about the key to happiness and success. But it is the consistent testimony of all who have tried it.

This is also a good guide to our practice of prayer. What many have found is that when we spend more time interceding for the needs and welfare of others and live with this type of cheerful, God-dependent self-forgetfulness, many of our needs and desires are met—even without asking.

So if you're grieving in this time of fear and confusion, how do these words of being a servant help you? It's counterintuitive, but true: Our pain starts to heal when we invest our lives in healing the pain of others—regardless of physical distance. When all our instincts tell us to hide somewhere and nurse our sorrow in solitude, the best medicine is to turn outward toward the brokenhearted around us and help them in their suffering. Try it—it works. And what enables us to truly care for (and feel) their pain is what we're going through now. It gives life profound meaning.

In the words of Pablo Casals, the great cellist, composer and conductor: "I feel the capacity to care is the thing which gives life its deepest significance."

What are some ways you can reach out today, sharing the gifts God has given you to bring hope and light to someone in desperate need of them?

PRAYER

Father, right now I'm unable to turn from my own pain and fear to that of others unless you grant me the grace and ability to do it. It's not in me, it's not part of my nature, so you must do it through me. Jesus made it clear

MY DAILY JOURNAL

AN IMPOSSIBLE WAY OUT

Rejoice always, pray without ceasing, give thanks in all
circumstances; for this is the will of God in Christ Jesus
for you.
-1 Thessalonians 5:16–18

There is another problem for victims of COVID-19—
besides having gone through the dreaded disease,
survived the intense fear of its outcome, and been able to heal
from it, people who have recovered now find themselves
facing the stigma of having had the virus. They are treated
like pariahs and find themselves targets of hate mail, *persona
non grata*.

Yvette Paz, a survivor of COVID-19 says, "The mental
drain of that has been just as tough, if not more so, than the
virus itself…. The overall message to the entire world is not
to lose our humanity…. We've lost our ability to empathize
and care for one another."[6]

Are you there now? Perhaps your or your loved one's lab
test results have just come in positive. Maybe you're stuck at
home in quarantine or have lost your job—you've worked
hard to find something else and there isn't any other
employment opportunity in sight. Or you're looking at your

empty bank account, your creditors keep calling, your investments took a down-turn and didn't turn out the way you expected; your family or marriage is falling apart, loved ones are in the hospital and you can't even be with them; you just don't know how you're going to make it through another hour, let alone another day.

If you think your situation is utterly impossible and beyond solution, then consider what the apostle Paul says in Romans 15:13 (NIV):

> May the God of hope fill you with all joy and peace as you trust in him, so that you may overflow with hope by the power of the Holy Spirit.

We all know what it's like to overflow with despair, disillusionment, or discouragement. But do you know what it's like to be bursting with hope, peace, and joy? You're barely getting through the day, and Paul talks about overflowing with hope? Forget it.

I hear you and can relate to what you're feeling. We have all been (or are) there. But remember, "hope" in the Bible bears no relation to how the world commonly talks about it. It doesn't mean "I hope so," but rather "I'm confident that...." It is connected to the character of God who is always reliable and who never loses his focus. The only real hope we have in this life or the next rests in God and his purposes. That's the first thing we need to know about hope.

The second is that our God is capable of filling us with peace and joy no matter what the circumstances. The Old Testament calls it "Shalom," a complete sense of well-being of both the spiritual and the physical, something found only in God's presence. We discover that we are generally healthier when filled with *Shalom*, and that we get sick without it. This gives us an indication of our design. We're meant for such a life and not for any other.

Third, this unique peace and joy come only as we trust in God—this is the difficult part. He imparts his *Shalom* to us as we lean on him and, through experience, find him totally sufficient for our needs (and many of our wants). This is what it means to trust him.

And finally, the result of this faith is that we can overflow with hope. It's not even a possibility outside the gift of God's presence with us. And that's the important point: all this occurs by the power of the Spirit. It's the greatest power in the universe. By it Jesus turned water into wine, calmed the storm, and raised the dead. The message of Jesus to us is not, "Please try harder, get better, and I'll do great things for you," but rather, "Lean wholly on me and my Father in your weakness and we'll make the impossible happen for you."

This is how we can be thankful this year, no matter what. God loves to do the impossible when we see no way out.

PRAYER

Loving God, I desperately need this kind of hope to get me through all that is happening. I can't create it or pretend that things are other than what they are. Real, overflowing hope is only yours to give. I ask you for this supernatural gift as you draw me close to you, and as you empower me to face the overwhelming odds against me. Grant also your inexplicable joy and divine fearlessness. Amen.

MY DAILY JOURNAL

_____

_____

_____

_____

_____

_____

_____

_____

_____

_____

_____

_____

_____

_____

_____

_____

THE ANTIDOTE TO A VERY BAD DAY

And we know that in all things God works for the good of those who love him, who have been called according to his purpose. For those God foreknew he also predestined to be conformed to the likeness of his Son, that he might be the firstborn among many brothers. And those he predestined, he also called; those he called, he also justified; those he justified, he also glorified.
–Romans 8:28-30

A
re you having a bad day? I mean a *really* bad day. Or maybe a long, endless stretch of bad days. Is that where you are?

Tsutomu Yamaguchi was no stranger to bad days. On August 6, 1945, the 29-year-old naval engineer with Mitsubishi Heavy Industries was completing a three-month work assignment in Hiroshima when the atomic bomb hit the city. Surviving the blast, Yamaguchi rushed to find a way to return to his family in a neighboring city. Fearing the worst, he passed horrifying scenes of carnage, and even had to swim in waters filled with layers of dead bodies to get to the train station, as the bridges had been blown away. To his relief, he arrived home to find his wife and baby safe and healthy.

Three days later, on August 9, 1945, Tsutomu, bone-weary and completely exhausted, reported to work. As he was recounting the events of August 6 to his disbelieving superior, for the second time in his life there was another iridescent light and deafening boom. The city Yamaguchi had returned to was Nagasaki, right as the atomic bomb hit.[7]

We'll pick up Yamaguchi's story at the end of the chapter. But for now, ask yourself again: Do you think that the terrible thing you're facing right now could turn into something good? Could it be one of the *best* things that ever happened to you?

The apostle Paul thinks so.

In Romans 8, Paul says that God is at work in everything for good for those who love God and are called according to his purpose. He even gives us examples in his own experience. In Philippians 1, he reminds us that being incarcerated in Rome actually served to further his mission, the whole reason for being there in the first place. And remember in 2 Corinthians 12, he says that God used a chronic physical problem to show him how the power of the Spirit works through our weaknesses. God exploits this world's evil to get his work done.

Paul also teaches in Romans 8 that God foreknows us, predestines us, calls us, justifies us, and then glorifies us in the end. This is the summary of God's purpose for us in this life and beyond. What this means for us is that he had his eye on us even before we were born (Psalm 139:1–18), and even before the foundation of the world.

He continues in Romans 8:31 by saying that if God is for us, and if we have been on his mind since even before the world was created, who could possibly be against us? It wouldn't matter if every person on earth became our enemy, God would still be all we need. Whoever accuses us or tries to define us, even if it's Satan himself, it means nothing. All that really matters is that God gives us his grace, forgiveness, and eternal glory in his presence. No one can take that away from us.

Finally, Paul reminds us that nothing, under any circumstances, at any time or in any place, could ever separate us from the love of God in Jesus Christ (Romans 8:35–39).

Nothing means nothing.

Name your greatest fear. God's love is still and always will be greater. Whatever we might fear could take us out of God's hands in this life or the next is forever trumped by his love for us. That's his last word over us.

Remember, it may take time, and it may take longer than we would wish. But this is a cutaway view of how life works for God's people, for all those who love God and are living for him. And it's not based on our greatness or excellence, but on God's. That's why it's good news.

The good news for Tsutomu Yamaguchi is that for the second time in his life, he survived—even surviving the effects of radiation and going on to live a long life. He became a translator for the U.S. armed forces during their occupation of Japan, went on to continue an engineering career at Mitsubishi, had two more daughters, and wrote poetry and a memoir. He even spoke before the United Nations, where he said, "Having experienced atomic bombings twice and survived, it is my destiny to talk about it."

So hang in there, and whatever you do, don't give in or give up!

PRAYER

God, I believe, but help my unbelief! It's difficult to see how the bad things in my life could turn out to be remotely good, but I know you love me and are working for me. It's so easy to misunderstand your plan for me. Clear away the confusion, and all false understandings and feelings that distort my vision of you. Settle my heart and mind with your peace. Grant me patience as you turn the bad into the good. Amen.

MY DAILY JOURNAL

ALWAYS IN GOD'S HANDS

This is the word that came to Jeremiah from the Lord:
"Go down to the potter's house, and there I will give you
my message." So I went down to the potter's house, and I
saw him working at the wheel. But the pot he was
shaping from the clay was marred in his hands; so the
potter formed it into another pot, shaping it as seemed
best to him. Then the word of the Lord came to me. He
said, "Can I not do with you, Israel, as this potter does?"
declares the Lord. "Like clay in the hand of the potter,
so are you in my hand, Israel."
–Jeremiah 18:1–6, NIV

My parents told me a story from one of their travels
that stayed with them for the rest of their lives. They
were in Eastern Europe in 1974 during the off season, so they
assumed that there would be plenty of hotel rooms available
for their stay. Arriving late at night, they discovered to their
dismay that there was a huge conference in the city and the
hotels were booked out.

Exhausted, they sat down on a bench near the
abandoned airport and prayed for God's rescue and
protection. Moments later, a stranger approached them and

asked if they needed help. When they explained their predicament, he took them in his car, drove them downtown to a beautiful hotel, and got them a room. The next day, he gave them a free tour of the city. They never knew what prompted this man to seek them out, but they knew from this experience that God was looking out for them, and they were safe in the hands of their Creator.

I wouldn't call this a miracle, but it's the kind of thing God likes to do to show us he is involved in every facet of our lives. This type of personal attention to detail is something God loves to use to communicate with us through our entire time on this earth. Sometimes it's something dramatic, but other times he chooses small, personal interactions to illustrate a point. In the Old Testament, when God chose to speak to his people Israel, he would often lead his prophet to some mundane scene from daily life, then give him a message using the details as a metaphor to make the message as clear and simple as possible. God didn't want the meaning to get lost in abstractions and complicated theology.

In Jeremiah 18:1–6, God wants the prophet to observe the potter as he fashions his vessel for some practical use. Just as the clay is totally dependent upon the potter, so are we absolutely dependent upon God. Since the potter knows what he's doing, the clay being shaped has no grounds for complaining or protesting about it.

In the same way that the potter has a design in mind for the clay, so God works according to plan for his people. There's no randomness in the shaping of the clay. There is good reason for the tools carving, scraping, cutting, and putting pressure on it. So there is intelligence and reason behind the hardship, grief, and difficulties (the shaping) God allows in our lives.

Just as the clay sometimes seems to resist the shape it's taking, so often we try to resist God's shaping of us. Israel consistently rebelled and did the exact opposite of what God wanted for them.

But the potter is persistent and often has to take the whole mass of clay, pick up the bits and pieces around the wheel, press them back into one lump, and start again. He doesn't throw out the whole thing and look for some new clay. God never gets so exasperated that he turns away and abandons his work. His patience in fashioning and refashioning eventually brings the vessel to its original design. Even Israel's (and our) mistakes are eventually shaped to accomplish his good and perfect will.

Paul writes in Acts 17:24–28 (NIV):

"The God who made the world and everything in it is the Lord of heaven and earth and does not live in temples built by human hands. And he is not served by human hands, as if he needed anything. Rather, he himself gives everyone life and breath and everything else. From one man he made all the nations, that they should inhabit the whole earth; and he marked out their appointed times in history and the boundaries of their lands. God did this so that they would seek him and perhaps reach out for him and find him, though he is not far from any one of us. 'For in him we live and move and have our being.' As some of your own poets have said, 'We are his offspring.'"

What Jeremiah's message in the Old Testament and Paul's message in the New Testament have in common is simply this: In the good times and the bad, we're always and totally in God's hands and in his providence. This means that how and where we are born, the place we live, how many years we exist on the earth, the trials we go through, including what's happening right now, and all the boundaries of our lives are in the mind of God.

He is in charge of all the gradual (even painful) shaping of our lives as well as the final product, intended for a practical and good goal. When the job is done, the beauty and form of the once formless clay brings pleasure, honor, and praise to the Potter.

PRAYER

Father, bring to the center of my mind what it means that you are totally sovereign, and that you are in complete charge of everything that happens, all the time, and in every life. Continue to shape me, the way you're doing right now, to make me the person you have put me here to be. Take away the illusion of randomness and chaos that tempts me to doubt you. Open my eyes to your presence, power, and love even when all the details of my life seem disordered and out of control. Thank you for what you are doing in me now. Amen.

MY DAILY JOURNAL

_____

_____

_____

_____

_____

_____

_____

_____

_____

_____

_____

_____

_____

_____

A MENTAL REVOLUTION

How sweet are your words to my taste, sweeter than
honey to my mouth! Through your precepts I get
understanding; therefore I hate every false way. Your
word is a lamp to my feet and a light to my path. I have
sworn an oath and confirmed it, to keep your
righteous rules.
–Psalm 119:103–106

I appeal to you therefore, brothers, by the mercies of God,
to present your bodies as a living sacrifice, holy and
acceptable to God, which is your spiritual worship.
Do not be conformed to this world, but be transformed
by the renewal of your mind, that by testing you may
discern what is the will of God, what is good and
acceptable and perfect.
–Romans 12:1–2

Baseball great Yogi Berra was well known for his witty,
no-nonsense philosophy, often referred to as "Yogi-
isms." One of my favorites is this: "When you come to a fork
in the road—take it!" How can you go wrong?!

For some people, this is about as good as human advice
gets when it comes to finding direction for life. But there is a

way to get God's direction for our lives, and his plan is the highest we could ever hope for.

In lockdown, most of us have had an abundance of time (whether we have wanted it or not) to think—to slow down, pray, assess our lives, and discover what's really important. This is also a good time for us to think and pray about what we are here on this earth to do. Why has God put you in the situation you are in? There is a reason for all of this.

So how do we go about finding it? The above passages from the Psalms and from Paul's letter to the Romans give us a good start:

1) **Begin with a renewed mind.** This is not just a change of mind, but rather a revolution of the mind. It's a complete change of our frame of reference. It means that whereas we usually tend to think that the entire world revolves around our wishes, our dreams, and our desires, we come to a place where everything revolves around the will of God. We orbit around him, not he around us. This is such a fundamental change that we can't make it happen ourselves. It must come from him. We can submit ourselves for transformation, but it's only God who can do the transforming.

2) **Get to know the Scriptures.** They are the counsel of God. They are a lamp to our feet lighting the pathway ahead. Don't know where to begin? Start with the Gospels. And then read the lives of Christians throughout history. They were

people who pored over the Scriptures daily seeking light and life.

3) Pray regularly for guidance and decide ahead of time that you're prepared to obey when God reveals the way for you. Begin and end your prayer with, "Not my will, but yours be done."

4) Move forward, searching while you wait (actively) for God's guidance. Don't stop and do nothing. Keep doing what you already know to do is right until God's new course for you is revealed. As the old saying goes, "A ship can be guided only when it's moving."

5) Consider all the factors: your dreams, skills, God-given gifts, things you love, and what God has blessed and prospered in your life before. Not always, but often, God guides us through what we really love and what makes our heart beat faster thinking about it. Even when we are led to do the unpleasant or the painful, there's a good end. Jesus didn't want to go to the cross, but the greatest event in history took place because of it.

6) Act in faith (trust), expecting God to lead in his way and in his time. Action is the only concrete form of faith. Worried you'll make a mistake? You probably will. So what? If we misread his guidance or stumble along the way, he can fix it and grant us a course correction. That's his job, not ours. Generally, our problem is not in being too aggressive in this respect, but in being too cautious or fearful.

If we look to God to find his purpose for our life, he is more willing to provide it than we are to receive it. And the action for us to take today is to begin actively searching out his will in Scripture and prayer, and to prepare to move when the pathway ahead lights up.

PRAYER

Lord, you are the only one who can completely rearrange my mind, my priorities, and my entire worldview. I earnestly desire this transformation. I want to spend my life from now on thinking your thoughts, speaking your words, and obeying your will. I know that this is absolutely impossible unless Jesus Christ does it all through me by his great power, in whose name I pray. Amen.

MY DAILY JOURNAL

HOW DO I KNOW GOD HEARS MY PRAYERS?

And this is the confidence that we have toward him, that if we ask anything according to his will he hears us. And if we know that he hears us in whatever we ask, we know that we have the requests that we have asked of him.
–1 John 5:14–15

How do we really know that God hears our prayers?[8] God's answers to many of our prayers are a complete surprise! I think that is the reason why we think he doesn't hear us, care about us, or has abandoned us. He works things out for our good—we just think we know what's good for us, and when we pray we expect him to respond to that particular request.

Here's one way I like to describe how we understand God's answers to our prayers. It reminds me of the ticket dispensers at a European railway station—scroll through, check the right boxes, put the correct change in the slot or swipe your credit card, and after a few whirrs, your ticket drops out into the bottom dispenser. You pick it up, well-pleased with your efforts, and you move on.

God isn't like that. There are no "5 Easy Steps" to get the answer you want. From his point of view, our prayers may seem painted in monotonous, boring shades of black and white. But the Creator of the universe responds in brilliant strokes of vibrant colors and dazzling patterns designed to reflect his glory and omnipotence. He is the God of the Impossible.

It's against this vivid and dynamic background that I would like you to consider your prayers and to recognize the way he has answered and answers them—in your favorite colors, tailor-made to help you understand that you are unique, his beloved child whom he created for the good road he has mapped out for your life.

The most interesting thing about God and the way he chooses to answer our prayers is that he loves the unexpected and the coincidental, even the humorous. He refuses to be predictable, except that we can predict with absolute certainty that he will be faithful and good. But we cannot tell exactly how he intends to answer our prayers, or when. He operates by plan, not by our wishes at the moment.

Often, when we expect A, he gives us B, in such a roundabout way that we observe the great personality behind the answer. We shouldn't be surprised at the highest intelligence in arranging and rearranging our circumstances, so that we marvel at the complexity, and the ease, with which he brings his solutions to us. He wants us to know that it didn't "just happen." It came from a brilliant Designer in a way, and at a time, that makes us laugh at his obvious flair for the dramatic. Why would it be any other way? He is God—not the God of our quaint, homemade theologies, but the all-powerful, sovereign deity of the Bible.

What about when we pray and then get a clear, heartbreaking no from God? What then? We can know that even in the face of a bewildering, echoing no, we will still find ourselves totally secure in the hands of God. Dr. Judith Briles tells us in her book *When God Says No* that one thing the Christian life teaches us is that behind every *no* there is a *yes*, if we wait for it.[9] If something we want or ask for isn't good for us, or if it drives us off course from his good will, God grants the *no* to our prayers just to keep us on course.

The whole world may be reeling from their fears of this pandemic, but there is nothing that confuses God or takes him by surprise. The things that shatter our plans, that bring us down to ground zero and make us start over in life, are but new opportunities in the hands of our Creator. It's time to celebrate God's deliverance right now, before it occurs! Get rid of that mythology that tells you, "All is lost" or, "There's no way out of this" or, "This is impossible!" And keep reminding yourself of this time-tested biblical truth:

> "Now to him who is able to do far more abundantly than all that we ask or think, according to the power at work within us, to him be glory in the church and in Christ Jesus throughout all generations, forever and ever. Amen."
>
> –Ephesians 3:20–21

PRAYER

Father, we are so thankful that it is impossible for you not to hear us when we pray, because you know and hear everything. We are grateful for your saying no to those things that would harm us. We humbly and firmly believe that behind the no is a yes. We pray for the grace to wait and trust, and to see your wonderful plans for us unfold according to your perfect blueprint and time schedule. Amen.

MY DAILY JOURNAL

CONCLUSION:
A NEW DAY DAWNING—
FEAR NOT

Fear not, for I am with you;
be not dismayed, for I am your God;
I will strengthen you, I will help you,
I will uphold you with my righteous right hand.
–Isaiah 41:10

In 597 BC, after the defeat of the Jews in Jerusalem, the Chaldeans herded them to Babylon, where they lived in utter despair. During this Babylonian exile, God spoke these words of hope to them: "Fear not, for I am with you; I will help you." These same words he speaks to us. We, too, can live without fear in a world full of fearful things, because he will help us.

God has already written out his life plan for us. The certainty of a glorious future that the people in exile didn't have, we have now in the knowledge of the living Christ. Dwelling in his Word, and with the help of his Holy Spirit, we grow into fearless believers. Keeping our eyes on the Perfecter and Bestower of our faith, we join the thousands who have boldly walked through every trouble and reached victory's shores hand in hand with him.

In each worry and anxiety, Jesus teaches us to lean heavily on our heavenly Father. And for those who call him Abba, this has been the guiding force sustaining their faith and trust—God's unfailing love.

Whatever we might be going through, people of faith have gone through it before, many times. As Solomon in Ecclesiastes says, "What has been is what will be, and what has been done is what will be done, and there is nothing new under the sun" (Ecclesiastes 1:9). So we turn to the history of God's people in the Bible and recall the testimonies of thousands who have lived through times of loss, grief, and persecution and survived to tell their faith stories to their children and grandchildren.

At the age of six weeks, Fanny Crosby, one of the most prolific hymnists in history who penned the beloved hymn "Blessed Assurance, Jesus Is Mine," caught a cold and developed an infection in her eyes. An unqualified doctor prescribed the wrong treatment that left her blind for life. She never once expressed resentment to a God who had dealt her such a blow. Instead, she wrote, "It seemed intended by the blessed providence of God that I should be blind all my life, and I thank him for the dispensation. If perfect earthly sight were offered me tomorrow I would not accept it. I might not have sung hymns to the praise of God if I had been distracted by the beautiful and interesting things about me."[10]

The powerful gift of God's trials to us is that they drive

us back to him. Adversity, hard times, and unexpected shocks are what awaken us to the knowledge that, thankfully, God is in charge and we aren't. It's often these dangers that lead us to safe haven.

How does a pandemic, or any disaster, become the vehicle that transports us to a haven? Well, as we gradually grow in our understanding of the Bible's message, we are much less shocked by life's surprises. We recognize them for what they are and say, Oh, this is from God. He wants me to ride this wave to shore and trust him as he leads.

Even though we may feel anxious at times, there's no need in the Christian life for dread, anxiety, or hand-wringing. Relying each moment on God's unfailing love, the Holy Spirit transforms us from fainthearted worrier to fearless warrior.

Let's gladly immerse ourselves in the joy of being loving and beloved children of the Most High—living loudly for God's glory and pleasure, celebrating what he has designed for our greatest good. So let us thank him for today's circumstances, no matter what they are, and rejoice knowing that he is in the midst of them.

Whatever the pain or confusion at the moment, by submitting ourselves to Jesus Christ our King and experiencing his goodness, we can live boldly, trust completely, and love joyfully. Inexpressible peace and confidence are what we have to gain, and anxiety and worry are all we stand to lose.

The abiding love of Jesus is what leads us forward from

deadly darkness to living light. This is our reason to live without fear amid the chaos around us, a truth stronger and more powerful than any disaster that comes our way—Jesus is ours. What a blessed assurance.

Nothing can ever separate us from him.

Perfect submission, perfect delight
Visions of rapture now burst on my sight
Angels descending, bring from above
Echoes of mercy, whispers of love
–*Blessed Assurance*, Fanny Crosby, 1873

ACKNOWLEDGEMENTS

Some families are spending time away from each other during this pandemic. I am very blessed that my family was able to return home just in time for us to shelter together. My thanks to my amazing wife, Shirin, and daughters, Sarah and Stephanie, for making life in lockdown a fun and faith-growing experience. Our many talks about God's love and mercy, and our focused times of prayer, led to the writing of this book. Thank you to Shirin for her encouragement to write this devotional and for taking time to go through my draft from start to finish, to Stephanie for her exceptional insights in editing, and to Sarah for her giftedness in completing the editing process to publishing. All three of them were vital in bringing this book to you.

ABOUT THE AUTHOR

JOHN I. SNYDER is an international pastor, conference speaker, and best-selling author of the books *Resenting God: Escape the Downward Spiral of Blame* from Abingdon Press, *Your 100 Day Prayer* from Thomas Nelson Publishers, and *Reincarnation vs. Resurrection* from Moody Press.

John has been featured on Focus on the Family, Moody Radio, Fox News, Faith Radio Network, Cru, American Family Radio Network, *In the Market with Janet Parshall*, *The Bottom Line with Roger Marsh*, Miracle Channel, *Bill Martinez Live*, and many more.

As an ordained Presbyterian pastor, John has served congregations in the United States and planted churches in California and Switzerland. He is currently pastor of Starnberg Fellowship, an international church in Bavaria. He is the advisor and lead author for theology and culture blog Theology Mix, which hosts 80+ authors and podcasters, and visitors from 175 countries. He received his Doctor of Theology degree magna cum laude in New Testament Studies from the University of Basel, Switzerland, where he studied with acclaimed professors Bo Reicke, Markus Barth, Martin Schmidt, and Jan Milic Lochman. He also has Master of Theology and Master of Divinity degrees from Princeton Theological Seminary in Princeton, New Jersey.

You can find his articles in academic journals, online magazines, and newspapers including *Theology Today*, *Theology Mix*, *Outreach Magazine*, *The Christian Post*, *Gospel-Centered Discipleship*, *Dialog*, *Theologische Zeitschrift*, *Journal of the Evangelical Theological Society*, *The Washington Times*, and more. John has also served on the adjunct faculty of New College Berkeley as well as the World Journalism Institute. You can follow him on Twitter @johnisnyder or connect with him on Facebook or LinkedIn.

NOTES

[1] John I. Snyder, *Resenting God* (Nashville: Abingdon Press, 2018).

[2] C.S. Lewis, *The Last Battle (Chronicles of Narnia #7)* (HarperCollins Narnia; Reissue Edition, 2007). Closing lines in Chapter 16: Farewell to Shadowlands.

[3] "Hymn Stories: God Moves in a Mysterious Way." Challies.com. https://www.challies.com/articles/hymn-stories-god-moves-in-a-mysterious-way (accessed September 2020).

[4] Project Wingman. https://www.projectwingman.co.uk/our-mission (accessed September 2020). "How the airline industry is coming together to support healthcare workers and how you can help too." Thepointsguy.com. https://thepointsguy.com/news/project-wingman-first-class-lounges-nyc (accessed September 2020).

[5] "Ebrahim Firouzi." Churchinchains.ie. https://www.churchinchains.ie/prisoner-profiles/ebrahim-firouzi (accessed September 2020). "An Update on Ebrahim Firouzi." Opendoorsca.org. https://www.opendoorsca.org/an-update-on-ebrahim-firouzi (accessed September 2020).

[6] "'Treated like a pariah': 11 COVID-19 survivors reveal what they want people to know." Today.com. https://www.today.com/health/coronavirus-recovery-stories-what-covid-19-survivors-want-you-know-t182607 (accessed September 2020).

[7] "The Man Who Survived Two Atomic Bombs." History.com. https://www.history.com/news/the-man-who-survived-two-atomic-bombs (accessed September 2020).

[8] I discuss the matter of daily prayer and waiting on God in my book *Your 100 Day Prayer: The Transforming Power of Actively Waiting on God* (Nashville: Thomas Nelson Publishers, 2011).

[9] Dr. Judith Briles, *When God Says NO: Revealing the Yes When Adversity and Pain Are Present* (Mile High Press, 2020).

[10] Fanny Crosby. Wikipedia.com. https://en.wikipedia.org/wiki/Fanny_Crosby#cite_note-christianhistorytimeline1-33 (accessed September 2020).

Made in the USA
Las Vegas, NV
03 December 2020